ILLUSTRATED EDITION

The Blue Day Book

A LESSON IN CHEERING YOURSELF UP

BRADLEY TREVOR GREIVE

Illustrated by Claire Keane

Andrews McMeel
PUBLISHING®

Other Books by BTG

Penguin Bloom

The World Is Great, and I Am Small

In Praise of Idleness: A Timeless Essay

Why Dogs Are Better Than Cats

Priceless: The Vanishing Beauty of a Fragile Planet

Curses and Blessings for All Occasions

The Book for People Who Do Too Much

The Meaning of Life

Tomorrow: Adventures in an Uncertain World

Other Books by Claire Keane

Little Big Girl

Once Upon a Cloud

Love Is

A Fairy Friend

To my wonderful parents, Fay and Trevor Greive,
who never stopped taking me out to see the world
even after I was bitten by penguins, three times.

BTG

INTRODUCTION

Much has changed in the past twenty years, but *The Blue Day Book* remains one of the simplest and most uplifting books you'll ever read. I'd love to say that you're about to be dazzled by wit and wisdom, but it actually contains nothing more than a humble, humorous lesson about perspective.

Writing this little book in the winter of 1998 helped me smile at a time when I needed it most, though of course I had absolutely no idea that it would eventually become the world's bestselling gift book of all time. I also had no idea that over the next two decades I'd undergo eighteen surgeries, almost lose my right arm, receive countless sutures, and endure five treatments for rabies, or that an enraged bull reindeer would try to tear off my left nipple. Life is full of surprises.

It's funny but also a little strange for me to recall the far younger and noticeably slimmer man who first conceived the idea that eventually became the book you hold in your hands. It's possible you may have enjoyed other books I've written since then, attended one of my lectures on creative thinking, or watched me track down giant bears and strange little creatures on Animal Planet . . . but long before I was a bestselling author, a public speaker, or a wildlife expert on television, I was a soldier. *The Blue Day Book* itself was born of honest desperation to understand how my life had become a dismal puddle of failure and disappointment following the sudden demise of my promising military career due to a tropical lung infection—just like that, my airborne beret and wings were taken from me, and if you only knew what it took to earn these, you wouldn't have to ask how much it hurt to lose them. And, worst of all, I could do nothing about it but weep tears of pain and rage, and then attempt to start my adult life over, from scratch.

After reinventing myself as a writer, I was determined to make a go of things—I worked hard and dreamed big, but somehow I never seemed to make any meaningful headway. My first book was rejected, as was my second, third, fourth, fifth, sixth, and seventh. The "thank you but no thank you" letters ran to dozens, then hundreds, rapidly filling up one dusty shoebox after another. I was barely surviving and became reliant on family and friends to get by. And then, after an especially rotten day, at the end of a tough week, in the middle of an awful month, during a very difficult year, I hit rock bottom like a concrete pancake. I was lonely and ill, my latest book had come to a juddering halt, I could not find a steady job or a steady girlfriend, and I was stupendously broke.

It's easy to allow bad luck and adversity to compound upon each other until pain and disappointment congeal into a fatal flummery of self-pity and hopelessness. We've all been there. Once, after feeling betrayed by a close friend, I lay on the living room floor in a wounded daze for three days, listening to "Honesty" by Billy Joel (from his fabulous *52nd Street* album) over and over and over again, on endless repeat. I still love Billy Joel, and this memory makes me laugh, but at the time I felt paralyzed by an overwhelming sense of my being infinitely unworthy and wholly unlovable. I was so frustrated and embarrassed by the miserable direction my life had taken and yet I only made things worse by running away from my problems.

The amusing, visual narrative you're about to read reinvents this experience in order to demonstrate how I finally found a way to turn things around. The fact that millions of readers have found it entertaining and helpful leaves me feeling humbled and also, somehow, less alone. It reminds me how much we are all alike, no matter how unique we think our personal misfortunes may be. But while I actively encourage literary critics to consider me a creative genius, I need to point out that the real turning point for me was simply a matter of taking the time to work through my thoughts and feelings on paper, and I readily admit that my greatest insight into how to overcome blue days may not ultimately amount to an intellectual ice cream headache.

While my challenges were very real, they didn't seem that bad when compared to the countless people who are truly suffering through no fault of their own, such as the wounded refugees I'd met when the army sent me to the Thai-Cambodian border in 1989. After comparing the scale and causes of my misery against my abilities and opportunities, it was clear I had every reason to be excited about what lay ahead of me. Then, having achieved something of a minor breakthrough, my mind started to wander and I began thinking about how wild animals deal with life's setbacks without access to cheap wine, group therapy, and Zoloft, and that's when I had a modest creative epiphany that made me laugh out loud. I decided there and then that I would do my best to share this private emotional journey and personal discovery with others. And here we are. In summary: I had some painful setbacks and I was feeling like crap, but when I really took stock of my life I realized it actually wasn't that bad, and thinking about a gloomy warthog taking psychotropic drugs made me snort-laugh. Obviously I wish I had a better superhero origin story, but I don't.

In the spirit of Billy Joel's "Honesty," let me come clean about three important things — I am not a psychiatrist, I'm far from perfect, and I'm no rocket scientist. Once I absentmindedly put an open packet of bacon in a kitchen drawer, instead of the fridge, where it sat, forgotten and putrefying, for several days. There are so many things that I have said and done over the years that I would take back or approach very differently if I had the chance again. But I'm not a quitter either. And by struggling on, and by learning from my mistakes, I have also learned to live with my regrets. I remain, in large part, the sum of my failures—and proudly so. Self-pity is the enemy of joy, and joy is an essential ingredient for anything worth doing. And so, for all my scars and flaws, I rather like being me. I've stumbled countless times, and I'm a misshapen work-in-progress, but despite my heart being shattered and pulped to crimson grease, I eventually found and married the love of my life. And despite years of unrelenting failure, I finally made it; this little book is proof of that. For all the blood and tears I've shed, I know I'm lucky to have lived a truly wonderful life-adventure, and I have the X-rays to prove it.

To those that accuse me of being a hopeful romantic and a starry-eyed reductionist, I do not disagree. I'm not against deep introspection, and I genuinely enjoy gazing up at the heavens while pondering the rich, vast, and complex fabric of human existence, but so often it's the little things that matter most. It's the endless little setbacks that finally break us, the fleeting gestures of kindness and moments of levity that lift our spirits, and the small personal victories that spur us on to far greater endeavors. For example, I once saw a drowsy, overfed Chihuahua fart so loudly that it jumped with fright and spun right around midflight, executing a perfect *tour en l'air*. Recalling this magical moment of pungent absurdity still helps me get through the most tedious domestic chores, professional obligations, and church sermons with a big smile on my face.

In the original *Blue Day Book*, my text was juxtaposed with stunning black and white wildlife photographs. However, this special illustrated edition has been completely reimagined by my incredibly gifted and accomplished artistic collaborator, Claire Keane. It was Claire's idea to create a new, central character to lead us through the book's narrative, and in the end she chose an elephant for this role, as she felt it best represented my large, clumsy, sensitive self attempting to navigate my difficult personal journey. Just as I wallowed in defeatist gloom as I struggled to get my books published, Elephant is often unable to get through each day, let alone achieve his seemingly impossible goal to appear on a Broadway stage. An outsider by every definition, for all his considerable might, Elephant is, at least initially, powerless to make his way in this oversized and overstuffed world. And I also like to think that by showcasing a literal elephant in the room, Claire offers us a visual subtext of personal loss, anxiety, sadness, and hopelessness that each and every one of us knows all too well, yet so few ever acknowledge.

Blue days are not easy to define, as each is so personal. Feeling blue can mean almost anything from a state of pleasant melancholy (think sexy French jazz on a rainy afternoon) to being completely disabled by corrosive, all-consuming depression. And if you are feeling depressed, please seek professional medical help as soon as possible—I would not be here today if I had not done this myself. With the right treatment you may be feeling much better far sooner than you imagine.

Look, I am not you. I have not experienced what you have, I have not seen what you have seen, and I don't pretend otherwise. But you can believe me when I tell you this: do not give up hope, and know that so long as you draw breath, hope will never abandon you. Also, take every chance you can to lighten the hell up—learning to laugh at your mistakes and misfortunes helps a lot. It doesn't mean the pain goes away, but at least it gets out of your way so you can move forward. Yes, life sucks sometimes, but if you can hold on until bedtime then you always have tomorrow to try again. It may sound trite, but sooner or later the key to your personal happiness and success will literally be just a day away. Also, it's always worth remembering that you happen to live on the only planet with flatulent Chihuahua ballerinas.

I can't easily express how overjoyed I felt, twenty years ago, when I grasped a freshly printed copy of *The Blue Day Book* with my eager paws; this visual work of fractured life philosophy was the eighth book I'd written, but my first ever published work. And yet I feel just as excited today, holding this fabulous new illustrated edition; it's funny and beautiful, and recalling the events that inspired this book still makes me laugh and also brings a few tears to my eye. I wrote the original for myself, but this one is for you. May it bring you joy, clarity, and comfort, and when times get tough, may it brighten your day and help remind you of countless reasons to smile.

Everybody has blue days.

These are miserable days when you feel lousy,

grumpy,

lonely,

and utterly exhausted.

Days when you feel small and insignificant,

when everything seems just out of reach.

You can't rise to the occasion.

Just getting started seems impossible.

On blue days you can become paranoid
that everyone is out to get you.

16

(This is not always a bad thing.)

You feel frustrated and anxious,
which can induce a nail-biting frenzy

**that can escalate into a
triple-chocolate-mud-cake-eating frenzy in the blink of an eye!**

19

On blue days
you feel like you're floating
in an ocean of sadness.

You're about to burst into tears
at any moment
and you don't even know why.

Ultimately, you feel like
you're wandering through life without purpose.

You're not sure how much longer you can hang on

It doesn't take much to bring on a blue day.

You might just wake up
not feeling or looking your best,

29

find some new wrinkles,

31

put on a little weight,

or get a huge pimple on your nose.

You could forget your date's name

or have an embarrassing
photograph published.

You might get dumped, divorced, or fired,
make a fool of yourself in public,

be afflicted with a
demeaning nickname,

or just have a plain old bad-hair day.

Maybe work is a pain in the butt.

You're under major pressure to fill someone else's shoes,

your boss is picking on you,

and everyone at work
is driving you crazy.

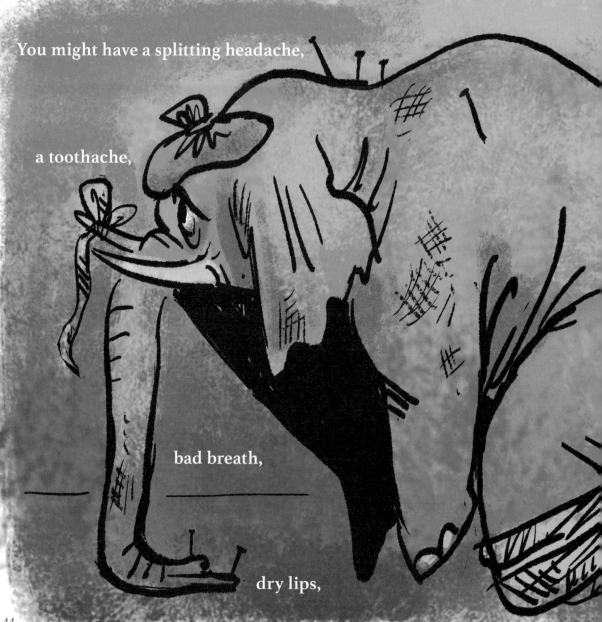

You might have a splitting headache,

a toothache,

bad breath,

dry lips,

44

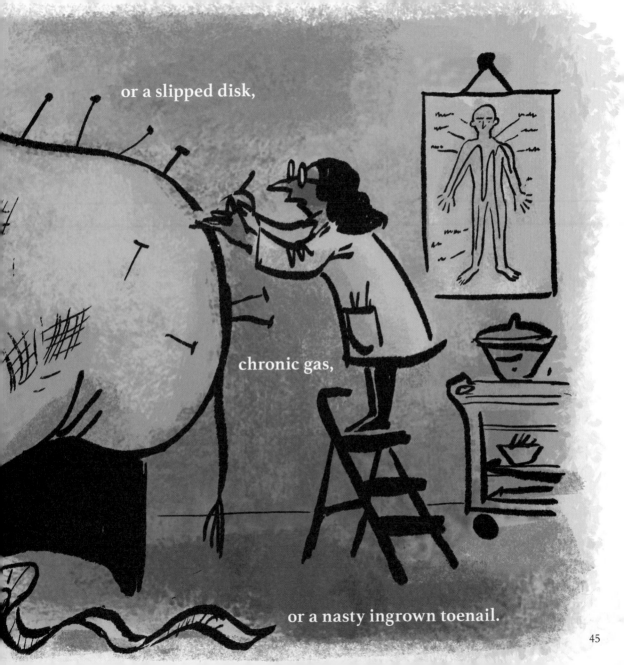

or a slipped disk,

chronic gas,

or a nasty ingrown toenail.

45

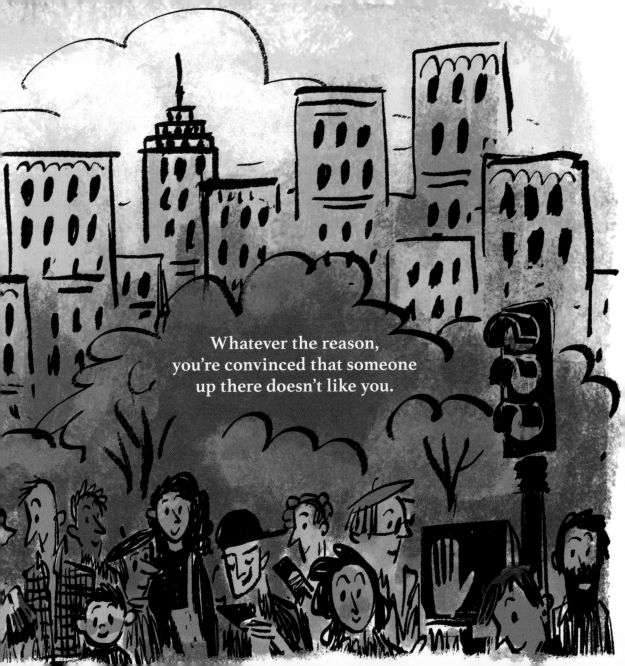

Oh, what to do, what to dooo?

Well, if you're like most people,
you'll do nothing but hide behind a flimsy belief
that everything will sort itself out.

Then you'll spend the rest of your life
waiting for everything to go wrong all over again.

All the while becoming crusty and cynical

or a pathetic, sniveling victim,

until you get so depressed that you lie
down and beg the earth to swallow you up

or, in the most serious cases, listen to Billy Joel songs on repeat until you achieve an altered state of consciousness.

This is crazy, because you
are only young once

and you're never old twice.

Who knows what fantastic things
are in store just around the corner?

After all, the world is full of amazing discoveries,

things you can't even imagine now.

There is fresh air aplenty, scrumptious snacks,
and magical moments to share.

Hey, you might end up fabulously rich

or even become a huge superstar . . . one day.

Sounds good, doesn't it?

There are cartwheels

and games to play

74

and yoga

and karaoke

75

and wild, crazy, bohemian dancing.

But best of all, there's romance.

Which means long dreamy stares,
whispering sweet nothings,

cuddles,

smooches,

more smooches,

and even more smooches,

a frisky love bite or two,
and then, well, anything goes.

So how can you find that blissful
"just sliding into a hot bubble bath"
kind of feeling?

It's actually pretty easy.

First, stop slinking away
from all those nagging issues.

It's time to face the music.

Now, just relax.
Take some deep breaths
(in through the nose and out through the mouth).
Try to meditate if you can.

Or go for a walk to clear your head.

Accept the fact that you'll have to
let go of some emotional baggage.

Try seeing things from a different perspective.

Maybe you're actually the one at fault.
If that's the case, be big enough to say you're
sorry (it's never too late to do this).

If someone else is doing the wrong thing, then step forward
bravely and say, "That's not right and I won't stand for it!"
When truth and justice are at stake, it's okay to be forceful.

Be proud of who you are

but don't lose the ability to laugh at yourself.

(This is a lot easier when you associate with positive people.)

Live every day as if it were your last,
because one day it will be.

Don't be afraid to bite off more than you can chew.

Take big risks.

Never hang back.

Get out there and go for it.

After all, isn't that what life is all about?

I think so too.

ACKNOWLEDGMENTS

In these last remaining pages, I wish to thank so many wonderful people, from all around the world, who have been instrumental in *The Blue Day Book*'s success. However, in the limited space that I have left, I can only give special mention to but a few luminous beings, starting with my beloved international literary agent, Sir Albert Zuckerman, of Writers House, New York; he is a true literary giant who plucked me from my home in Tasmania and plopped me down on the world stage, and then, some sixteen years later, was also the celebrant at my wedding in the Santa Monica Mountains.

I remain eternally grateful to my original editors, Christine Schillig (USA) and Jane Palfreyman (Australia); after countless rejections, they were the first publishing heavyweights to believe in the potential of this strange little creation. And for this latest incarnation of *The Blue Day Book*, I wish to thank Patty Rice (USA) and Brigitta Doyle (Australia), who are both wonderful creative allies.

My Australian literary agent, former publisher, and dear friend Jeanne Ryckmans was a huge champion of this new edition, as was Claire Keane's agent, Steven Malk, of Writers House, San Diego. And of course this book would never have happened at all were it not for Claire's immense talent and wonderful sense of humor, which have made our creative collaboration such a joy.

To each and every bookseller who personally recommended *The Blue Day Book* over the past twenty years, I thank you from the bottom of my heart. And to every booklover who purchased a copy for themselves and/or for someone special—especially friends, colleagues, and loved ones who were enduring difficult situations—I am truly grateful for your support, and I hope that this little book has given you, and those you care about, the same tiny jolt of joyous optimism that it gave me when I first wrote it.

My personal philosophy of pragmatic cheerfulness is largely the result of lessons taught to me by my family, my teachers, and a few terrifying drill sergeants, as well as all the friends, mentors, and wild creatures I have met throughout my wonderfully injurious life adventure. Whether pleasurable or painful, I am grateful to every single encounter for offering me new experiences, challenges, and perspectives that have made my life richer.

And finally, above all, I wish to thank my darling wife, Amy, whose loving example daily inspires me to be my best self. You make me far happier than a broken-down soldier, held together by titanium bolts and scar tissue, ever deserved to be. You are every star in my sky, you are the fire in my heart, you are my home.

Andrews McMeel Publishing
a division of Andrews McMeel Universal
1130 Walnut Street, Kansas City, Missouri 64106

www.andrewsmcmeel.com

19 20 21 22 23 SDB 10 9 8 7 6 5 4 3 2 1

ISBN: 978-1-4494-9029-4

Library of Congress Control Number: 2018961488

ATTENTION: SCHOOLS AND BUSINESSES
Andrews McMeel books are available at quantity discounts with bulk purchase
for educational, business, or sales promotional use. For information,
please e-mail the Andrews McMeel Publishing Special Sales Department:
specialsales@amuniversal.com.